Inheriting Craziness Is Like a Soft Halo of Light

everyone's got one but no one can see it

Poems

Thomas Fucaloro

THREE ROOMS PRESS

NEW YORK CITY

Several poems in this volume have previously been published, including:
"Ode to my Dad's Porno Mags"—published in *you say. say.* (Uphook Press, 2009)
"Married to Divorce"—published in *Nomad's Choir.*
"Ode to the unemployed and their mother's couches"—published in *poetz* (www.poetz.com).

Inheriting Craziness Is Like a Soft Halo of Light: everyone's got one but no one can see it

Cover:
Photos: Rod Morata (www.rodmorata.com)
Design: Rodolfo Leyton (www.rodolfoleyton.com)

Interior and Additional Cover Design:
Kat Georges (www.katgeorges.com)

First Edition

Printed in the United States of America

ISBN: 978-0-9840700-7-7

Printed in the United States of America.
Text set in Aldus

Published by
Three Rooms Press, New York, NY
threeroomspress.com

THANK YOU

To the family I love:
My mom and dad and sister Lauryn.

To the never ending influence of:
Jane Ormerod, Brant Lyon, Ice, R. Nemo Hill, Bob Heman,
Bob Hart, Jay Chollick, Peter Carlaftes, Ryan Buynak,
David Lawton, Obsidian, Hobo Bob, Elliot D. Smith,
Jared Singer, Jon Sands, Jive Poetic, JeanAnn Verlee,
Emily and Geoff Kagan Trenchard, Shappy and
Cristin O'Keefe Aptowicz, Jacob Victorine, Rock, Catharsis,
Nadia Bourne, Jahnilli Akbar, and to the other poets
I did not mention you know my heart swells.

Without these musicians and poets I wouldn't be:
Mike Patton, the Melvins, the Beatles, George Carlin,
Richard Pryor, Bill Hicks, Charles Bukowski, Ginsberg, Kerouac,
and of course my flower ee cummings.

A heartful thank you to:
Rodolfo Leyton and Rod Morata
for helping me to realize the insanity of the cover.

Very special thanks to:
Three Rooms Press and Kat Georges
for her undying patience and faith in me.

This book is dedicated to:
Josephine Fucaloro—who taught me how to be gentle
and
Phillip Barbera—who taught me how to be Thomas

CONTENTS

OATMEAL AND HEINEKENS

slurped up spine break
the luscious green bodies know
I've drank from them for far too long

this resemblance to Thomas

I could never quite perfect the hair
and tumble roar screech sets the initial
winding of time to a noon you can really
believe in

when you've been drinking
since your grandmother was born
you kind of notice equilibrium is a virtue
a loving song spurs bright a melody
that can only be heard by blowing
in empty bottles of Heineken

you wonder far too often for the beer to keep up
so you realize the importance of recyclable trash.
the importance of the first page but by the tenth
you realize poems just aren't as beautiful as
sunrises.

THANK YOU

Thank you so much. This is such an honor. Wow.
I'd like to thank the other Golden Globe nominees.
Umm, I'd like to thank the Academy, I'd like to thank
insert your name here for always believing in me and
I'd like to thank the skies on my TV for being so inspirational
and I'd like to thank tumors for they are truly the new gods
and I'd like to thank the Osmonds for being with us for so long
and I'd like to thank poems for helping me find god
  and understanding
you don't have to shake its hand and I'd like to thank
  teen sex trends
because I know that's the result of some sort of chart
and then those feelings are interpreted into questions that
  are given
to focus groups primarily accountants and they turn
  those answers
into a self help book on parenting and I'd like to thank
computers for killing the video star and I'd like to thank
the Coalition For Sanitizing Holy Water Order.
Such good work they're doing, with everyone dipping
their dirty fingers in the same holy water basin
it's like a germ pool and I'd like to thank commercials
that show sick children, dogs and kittens and I'd like to thank
the remote control and the Osmonds are spreading
and I'd like to thank heaven for without you where would I go
and I'd like to thank no struggle, no life affirming stories,
  no lessons
leaned and I'd like to thank Teen Sex Trend Wednesday Nights
at the Hustler Club, primarily accountants and they are spreading
and if you die in heaven then where do you go

and I'd like to thank William Carlos Williams.
He has been such a true friend through everything
but no one has ever been truer than my imaginary
bestest friend in the whole wide world, Thomas.

SO LET ME GET THIS STRAIGHT

"So let me get this straight,"
the editor of *People Magazine* said

"you want us to publish a cover story on you
for being a poor traveled, pot smoking, no sensed, lego haired
poet with a big nose." It's more like a slope I thought.
"Please gives us a reason to even consider this?"

A long pause felt right.

"Because the leaves of the trees said so."

Then he asked, "How the fuck did you get into my office?"

"Poetry baby.
 It's poetry."

IN A LONG MISSILE INTO FOREVER GOES THE MOON

and a new sun appears
because we know there can't be just one sun.
It's a con. The government can't control health care
but they do control the sun. It's either them or the Japanese.

That's why I always close my shades

to allow a little of my own light in.

PINK

I slap the wall above the doorframe

and you think intermediate school.
You think hair gel and Kaveritches
and some sort of proof you're a man.
Above the doorframe might do.

I guess Community College saved my life.
It brought me cummings and Ginsberg and
Donner and Blitzen and showed me how
to imitate Bukowski to a T-h-o-mmmmmmmmmmm
there's nothing funny about alcohol abuse
then why am I always smiling
wishing upon those stars

and then I slap the wall above the doorframe

get on up, besides the abuse and the influences
I've started growing a beard to make my poems better.
The beard phase of the poet. Their prime.
Even Emily Dickinson went through this.
It's all downhill . . .

there's nothing funny about sobriety
then why am I always laughing at sober people.

I slap the wall above the doorframe.

I can't tell you how many poems I have about pink hippos.
What I try to do sometimes, to write sober, is meditate
on a mantra for my poems hence, pink hippos, perfectly sober.
But then they start popping up in my unsober poems

and I slap the wall above the doorframe.

There's nothing funny about drug abuse

then why am I always
writing

about
pink
hippos.

AMERICA'S DEPENDENCY ON OTHER PEOPLE'S MISERY

On the TV
an alcoholic father
sells his 4 little girls
for $15,000.
The world today.
The craziness
to think that $15,000
means much

I mean with the dollar down and gas prices soaring and milk prices soaring and the puzzlement is soaring, why didn't this man try to get a better deal? It sounds like a lot of money but in the end, with what we have today, tomorrow is not looking brighter. He should have tried to sell them separately, not as a set. But hey, I guess that's the older generation and their mind set. My generation would have definitely negotiated a better deal, we're much better at bullshit I've noticed for example, I write poems. As far as the younger generation, they would have killed the kids and just invested in real estate. It's a strange world out there and I'm just a retail poet just trying to get through it. Or break through it. Or understand

how an alcoholic father
could sell his 4 little girls
for $15,000
and why can't I turn off the TV
and stop taking all these pills
the green ones
the oval ones
the indent in the middle ones
the orange ones
the store at 25 degree Celsius ones

the yellow ones
the protect them from moisture ones
the keep this out of the reach of children ones
the capsule ones

(the ones to help me write this poem)

the keep this out of the reach of poet ones
the smurf ones
all lead me to believe
I'm miserable too
just not on the telly.

I WALK INTO YOUR MIDNIGHT HOPING FOR MY OWN SUN TO RISE

I am desperate to sleep.
Maybe it's just that I've been trying to stay away from my dreams.
Night beat influence should know I don't know no better.
Without perfection you have humanity.
Without humanity, the left and right cerebrum of the sun
is beset on all sides.
The moment we touch is worth hoping for.
Shout a splendor so pure it can't help but feel the notion
of open spaces so warm
touching on the verge of building ledges.
The sun boils between my ears.
It's wisdom until you're eaten.
I've been swallowed up in my room for weeks now
on the verge of ledges and open wires of wrists.
She came in through the bathroom window or the bedroom
or whichever window you choose
on the verge of building ledges
leaning, just right.
The chilled night air
is nothing more than unfulfilled oceans
of ourselves.

MEDICATION

The disillusionment of cells
about the breaking together, coming apart
this cynic in me
has to agree
those rough seas ain't what they used to be.
They're plosive
then fallowed out hollowed out plowed for no discover.

The disenchantment of cells
forming new bases to be
forming new bases to begin again
forming new bases to be gin and tonic and it is only write
  to want to discover
what ticks and what ain't.
Usurp the movement of air to sitar that feeds on energy
  fiending light
or some other abstracted form
freeing the temples with rain
and reign on the pulse to the east fading a pale yellow brown almost
dried up
leaves.

THOMAS, THE SURGEON

Paging Dr. Thomas, Dr. Thomas please.

They need my assistance.

I hope I don't have to take out another liver or spleen,
bile takes forever to come out. It is a liver removal, ok
nurse, I need wooden spoons, an esophagus and a pear.
We're going to make a new liver for this man oh and nurse,
can you get me my pills? They help sober me up.

ELEPHANTS ARE HANGING FROM CRANES

Poets are hanging from cranes
trying to get there
large husk hide
flowing write
hangs there
floating
ocean seeps their cries
dark husk thick
ample needs
crane tac toe
marsh feeling romance
roaming the stomach
suck—
such x-o-x-o-x-o blunt repair
of a kiss
a hold
hangs over
fallen rusted husk hide.

And the crane aches
the word creeps
and we are the beats below.

COKE, THE ULTIMATE WHITE GIRL

(From a conversation with Robert Gibbons)

She got me hooked
line and head back mucus blend infinite
rush ascends another waking
hour without a poem. Who
wants them anyway?
Needle nose plyer guy thought spirals the sanctity of this
   soft single sigh . . .

This white pony broad
appeal of your waist during the spring time.
It's got me slapping asses
and slipping thighs anything
but a truth.

But them white girls them white hipped heel death girls rattle
   soft soliloquy silent . . .
Letting another afternoon pass head back, nose high
and my poem is a poem because it only tells the truth when
   you want it to
but it is scared of me.

My poems have become afraid of me lately.
They're running from me.
They're afraid
and the simple arithmetic line break thing appropriate
now
write what's on the other side.

THE 80'S

...and he rose from the ashes of millions of digested jelly beans.

I haven't spoken to him since I was 11, now he visits every night.

Hollywood actors who become governors and then become
presidents and then become stamps and then become
commemorative plates are what they have to offer.

During his economic up-h*evil* he helped my parents get me
Nintendo
and he helped many a businessman's balls get shinier with beautiful
blondes with really really big tax incentive plans.

Some say his love was Nancy, I say it was a generation's
hole sphincter
that saw the most love.

Ronald Reagan speaks to me when I am on the toilet, he says,
trickle down.

He says no to hugs. He says potato chips. He says the standard
of living
will only get better. He says eat before you go swimming.
He says I have
nice hair. I wear his pain, falling through each strand

and he replies ROGAINE. ROGAINE.

ODE TO THE UNEMPLOYED AND THEIR MOTHER'S COUCHES
OR
BEING UNEMPLOYED GAVE ME ENOUGH TIME TO WRITE LONGER POEMS
OR
IT'S HARD TO FIND THE TIME TO KILL YOURSELF WITH YOUR MOTHER NAGGING YOU ALL THE TIME

Settle down, settle down my throat and numb.

Two six packs a day keeps the jobs away.

My bladder is small but my will is good.

Often time is a wrist watch not yet wound for worry.

I say save the rats, we're gonna need them

to remind us we all live in the holes in our walls.

Licking the spit of an everyday couch speeds up

the possibilities of darkness and breathes.

I see people on TV praying at sporting events.

I wonder if this works . . .

Dear Jesus
won't you please do my dishes?
Won't you scrub them hangnail clean?
Jesus I want a new shower curtain
because I used the last shower curtain
to put out that fire on my stove and Jesus
why can't the beings in ourselves
create a sense of wonder screaming
for some semblance of what that pit
in my stomach is or is it a seed and Jesus
can you get some toilet paper while you're out

and Jesus can you beat me with a hammer
to see the light in your eyes and Jesus
can you make it so my coupons don't expire
and Jesus will you pass me the remote
and Jesus if I'm the image of god
can you pray to me and Jesus
does it matter if you cross your fingers
and Jesus why is Paul Mooney on Dr. Phil
and Jesus when will you realize what a great
fucking poet Eliott D. Smith is
and Jesus can you find me a job?

Sometimes I need to be held.

I go find my mother and give her a hug.

I used to think cigarettes were healthier than my parents

but this embrace

this embrace right here is the ocean of possibilities

brewing from a mother and son shakes the foundation

I thought I stood on but then I realize

my foundation is hugging me back.

THE LONELINESS OF SOME POEMS
OR
HOW TO SOUND LIKE A ROCK SONG FROM THE 70'S
OR
I'VE GOT THE BLUES, I'VE GOT THE BLUES OF YOUR EYES TO GET ME BY
OR
ANOTHER TYPICAL THOMAS POEM

I don't understand
Thomas
Neruda in Spanish
the pope
Jesus
industrial waste

cocaine.

I don't understand the laundry
but I do it anyway and I have learned
to breathe underwater

cocaine.

I don't understand
tupperware
beauty contests
Hanna Montana hand sanitizer

cocaine.

I've learned the solitude of the eternal
hum and I just stare at the fabrics going
tumble dry. I'm getting better at understanding
the laundry

cocaine.

I don't understand
Betty Crocker
Winston Churchill (the Camel Light years)
hydroglyercin
e.e. cummings (but that's the beauty of him)
lilies
camera phones

cocaine.

I don't understand the metaphysics of an embrace
always a character I wanted to play in reel life.
There's no Gap clothing in this washing machine
none, except the ones I stole out of my roommate's closet

cocaine.

I don't understand
Russian poets with French accents
Strom Thurman
Herman Munster
string cheese
old blues poets played at '45 speed

cocaine.

I understand that I understand less and less
'cause my head keeps smacking the floor more and more
but I've learned control—snort a few crushed vicodin first.
I think my dog is worried about me

cocaine.

Understanding's not a problem anymore
neither is the laundry. I kicked the shit
out of that rooster a long time ago

cocaine.

I thought I found the embrace but she decided to be in someone else's poems.

MOST LOVE POEMS DESERVE REQUIEMS

They deserve to die indeed

and become a bag of Skittles.

I like Skittles. They are bite sized candy.

So is love.

I always bite one before eating another

but your thighs softly assume this infinite madness to an extreme

haunts my back

and neck meet to write this growl

at the things that hold me

and the growl for the things holding me together
like parentheses—

linoleum tiles

standing me up

this feeling of a small baby crawling kitchen bound.

I kneel down

and tickle its feet.

THOMAS, THE SURGEON

Delivering babies is difficult
especially FedEx because sometimes
they don't have shipping boxes so you
have to use those soft envelope things
and it's always difficult to get the baby
to cooperate to place the FedEx label
on it but once complete, family is of
our utmost importance when mailing
a loved one home.

GIVE ME A 10 EVEN THOUGH I FEEL LIKE A 3

I'm a great person
when my good person
allows me to be great.

Tangled up in preservatives
reconcile past discoveries
of heart and food coloring.

When you mention Jesus in your poems
you get high scores
but only from the judges.

Peeling tangerines is easy
and worth the nectarine
mango madness buffet.

You know when you
know you know and
I know the middle of nowhere.

It's the center of everyone
peeking, pilling it
just a little bit.

I never read from the paper.
It is always reading
from me.

Claustrophobic
witch doctor demons
are the least of my worries.

Learning the violin
seems easy. Learning
the learning seems hard.

Privy pits preserved
because we like that
historic shit.

I find it intoxicating
when urinating
by candlelight.

When you use this kind of
tone in your voice it sounds
like you're really saying something.

Can't give respect to someone
who doesn't put time and thought
into their lies.

Poetry the next
hustle. Hustling
the next great poem.

At school kids go through
emotional damage when texted, you're ugly.
I just used to get beat up.

If you position your incision
through my bones
I won't have to rewrite your poems.

Bob the beating Hart of New York
blooms a brussel of cool
calming tides of breath.

Vicodin, vicodin
stop letting us in.
We keep knocking.

Trying to impersonate my voice
in all these poems
wrinkles the bark and leaves.

Learning to keep my hands
to myself but never my heart,
pass that motherfucker around.

I know you didn't call
but it's nice to think
that you did.

I've been trying to burn
hopeless into art because
less hope writes the richest sonnets.

The more I die
The better
my poems
become.

ODE TO MY DAD'S PORNO MAGS

My first wrong insight at what a woman should be
but an insight none the less
under your bed
who knew such wisdom would lie
dictating who you were
and who i was meant to be.
A page turner.
A bible salesman.
An escaped heart
flow
pours more into an ocean of never and remove
the pressure
boils over the mountains of flessshhh toned glistened pages
upon pages
of abstract women in reality based nude
          these economic times
          and my mind swells.
What will my therapist think 30 years from now when i let
   him know
i don't need to talk
just medication
maybe some meditation
under a bed, bare
of what a woman should be
and the flow pours more into an ocean of never

a rush, streams
          through

like a decent airline
and the female passengers
all say, "Fuck me next!"

and the invitation
becomes my heart.

That's what all the ladies want
          some hard heart
          some thought
                    less eyes
          some cranial shifts
          between the thighs

and the flow pours more into an ocean of never
and your dad's porn mags are now my heart
but what about love?

And the flow pours more into an ocean of never.

I'M AFRAID TO WRITE A POEM ABOUT YOU

so I'll just kiss your inner thigh instead.
Sullen moonbeam shouts out the darkness
softening every kiss to the playfulness of the tongue
licks hallelujah woman holding me thigh tight
and I say hallelujah to villanelles and sonnets
helping me get the rhythmed rhyme write.

Her heart, marble washed studded stone
ready for the cracks
of this broken down poet monsoon pile
of demeanor.

Wanna buy a noun
of the insect variety
crawling along the verbiage
lady buggin' me to flutter on.
Your praying mantis fantasies are vermin to me
vermin, with a twist of your thighs

I remember

to always pick pieces of your hair and thickness

from out of my teeth

and my poems.

POLKA DOT RIPE HEART BEAT APPEAL

of indigenous becoming
the new fashion craze. Indigenous
goes well with white and green Nike's
and you wonder how long the world
will take to unravel this ball of yarn
yearning to be a warm spring blanket
in the twilight of May or shall it become
an organic t-shirt or an organic hand bag
are still made from organic 5-year-olds
in Korea and you wonder why all this
fuss about revolution, alchemy, reason
just circle this cosmos with an
oh zone baby, ooooyeah, that ohh zone.

ISN'T THE RAIN BEAUTIFUL MIRRORED IN ALL LIVING THINGS, CRAWLING

bead drop after beat drop and turn
round and around the tongue knows.
it always knows. the best nights to remember
looking at it through the leaves of the trees
little green tongues dancing with the breeze
licking the clouds in my sky and a moment
of silence for photosynthesis ______________.
I admire you photosynthesis and the way
you always allow me to breathe
in
her
moments
and cry out a light
candle bound.

HERE I AM, 32, OLDEST I'VE BEEN SO FAR

But only wiser between
soft patterns of breath part the little hairs where the
earlobe and neck meet. You place your pulse there
as our lips tremble. We find our hopes there.
In that one tiny spot
such knowledge lies that we often only mistake for pleasure.

THIS IS ABOUT THE ECONOMY
OR
(NAKED PICTURES OF YOU)

Love does not conquer all

but it conquers enough

and I realize you were just another sonnet to get sex to me.

To hold me. To hesitate only if poems require a more mental
mortal touch.

Boobs, booze, it's all relative. Jamie Martin once said to me,

"If you buy my chapbook you're helping me eat."

Well if you buy pills from me you're helping me drink

and then you feel like a paraplegic in love and on the verge

of a horizon.

You stem well need more blossoms in your life
but when you're on your hands and knees throwing up at Bar 13
flowers often anoint themselves dead. I'm getting 'em young
in my old age and you weren't interested in saving me anymore
and I wonder what time the healing shall begin? We were never
meant to be but you were still my coke-con-spirit-tor racking
the rocks up chopping 'em down the soft curve of your middle back
entices a blossoming of spelling my last name out and then using
your bellybutton as a cup with a straw in it and you simply didn't
care as long as you got the next line and it's not that difficult to
rhyme machete with poetry when trying to slice my soul back and
there's not enough mucus in my poems so I get another bag and race
to the pen and fall to the floor and realize

I am alone. Jobless. Witless. Without gills, just need the funds
to stay afloat.

I sell naked pictures of you to prison inmates on the internet.
I sell naked pictures of you to dealers in my neighborhood.
I sell naked pictures of you 'cause my poems don't know no better.
I sell naked pictures of you 'cause my heart don't beat no better.

WHEN WE KILL

we leave the children alive for revenge purposes.
It's importing and exporting goods.
Assassinate a king, a queen, a dictator
leave the kids so they one day attack back
and this helps stimulate the economy
and that's why I think cheerleading should be a sport.

NOT IN A SEXUAL WAY

My parents have been divorced for over twenty years
but my mom is still in love with my father
who's been in 2 marriages twice removed
but that's another teen angst poem by a 32 year old for another time.

Parents see themselves in their kids
and when I look in the mirror I see my mom, dad, me
 monstrosity morph
a crooked nose who has a disposition to recite his woes like
 childhood poems
to others and their childhood poems understand my woes
 and they drink
way too much together
but still understand.

Well could one of you explain it to me . . .

in a fortune cookie or a good kick to the ribs

as much as I try to veer this poem in a different direction
I can't escape the feeling that my mother falls in love with me
every time
my father resonates.

STARTIN' TO HAVE SOME ISSUES WHERE I CAN'T SEPARATE THE DRUGS FROM THE POETRY

I think i remember but i think in

amnesia terminology

long taught by the Aztecs

but i remember the lines on the page

the way that pen glided across the margin of the horizon

i small compared to it

To know it. To now it. Into this moment

i becomes a poetic god-like-creature-thing with horns and

paws and misspelled words and i cant's remember the name

of this reapture or its function and i repeat, rise, respond

with such harsh craze that stigmatic cyclones thrust forth

in the palm of your tiny hand but you are no martyr

just a below average poet who can't commit himself

without a little drink

without a little drug

without a mourning swig

without a morning sunrise

without making mistakes.

I realize it.

i count on it.

The poem counts on it.

This next line understands it.

(A SEX CHANGE POEM)

It's interesting that bars have to have signs up telling pregnant
women not to drink

Like Stevie Wonder sings, "The writing's on the wall."
And I am superstitious and believe that the sign probably
should be there.
I'm sitting here just drinking probably trying to look for
a reason to read that sign
but my wine wonders off
into the sparkle of my eyes
smothers it.
Lets it ripple an extension that supersedes the ultimatum of you
ordering another bottle and you really start talking to your drink
explaining the things to come and the things to be
and I betcha I can crumble just like the next woman.

THE SKY HAS NO FORMAL EXCUSE

I always have the weapons but nothing to kill.
Nothing living inside that just wants to break out

and touch another human being with a knife
or a hatchet or a pop song or apathy or a parent.

What do you do when your parents don't respect you?
Write poems about them

but are parents the problem or is it the kids?
Harlem is going to be the new Times Square

in ten years and I wonder why I've killed nothing
just let it rest and it did all over.

I nut Harlem all over the place hoping
it stays Harlem. Did you know Nestles' makes bottled water?

That should have been my first kill.
But I just took a sip and moved along

watching the migration of cell phone elbows
up and down the block. I get cell phone elbow

when I jerk off
like celebrities on talk shows.

Why is it courageous for celebrities to get diseases?
My grandfather's not on Entertainment Tonight

talking about the fact that he's not fully covered
by the bed sheets in the home he died in, alone.

Maybe that, was my first kill.

MOTIVATIONAL SPEAKER FOUND STABBED (THE MEANING OF MOTIVATION)

I always applaud death
you never know when she may be in the room
and you never know if the room comes with twin beds
or you're just fucking each other.
Fucking the living death
would be wondrous indeed
and round shoulder blades feel
like the smoothest solid ocean
ready for the pulse of a new waterway
submerged in all this death

rising.

WHATEVER DISEASES BROOKLYN HAS
IT CAUGHT FROM STATEN ISLAND
OR
THE STATE BIRD IS THE MIDDLE FINGER
OR
POEMS GET YOU SO WRAPPED UP
IN WHO YOU WANT TO BE
THAT YOU OFTEN FORGET WHO YOU REALLY ARE

The ever so often visiting my mom in Staten Island
for years and visiting Brooklyn for less as Staten Island
wants to be Brooklyn so I say I'm from Brooklyn.

No matter how much neighborhoods change
streetlights remain the same.

The longest season is the heart unkempt but often.

I always thought the hypnotic heartbeat of hope
was in my heart but it's really in my mother's eyes.

Staten Island is man-made and man-made is natural.
Nature hums a rattled 'jacent bloom.

When you lose your mind in Staten Island it always
comes up Nabisco cracker crunch exuberance of
beautiful trees and hair gel.
You need to know where the cracks in the sidewalks are
and the assholes and how to get to the nearest branch.

Paul McCartney and Stevie Wonder sing
"There is good and bad in everyone . . . "
Then why this rotting corpse of a poem?
Then why this rotting borough of New York?

The longest season is my mother's eyes.

But now I'm under Harlem's gaze
her eyelashes
her soft whispers around my neck
providing a hope of what's next.

What's a possibility of light without Harlem?

No matter how much the neighborhood changes
my heart remains the same.

I always thought the hypnotic heartbeat of hope
was in my mother's eyes but it's right here.

Everywhere is where I see in you.

Thomas has lived in Harlem for ten years
but Harlem has lived in me my whole life.

I was born for it.
I may lose it.
I may have to move back to Staten Island.
I may have to stab my self in the neck
with my mom's medium sized wooden spoon.
I may have to pronounce the word the—da
as in can I get da door for you or da Beatles
or da night blooms over da margin's horizon
plumaging in da late day sun.
I may have to say I'm from Brooklyn.
I may have to dream without light
without conga drums
without dominoes
without families.

Longing, it's the longest of all seasons.

PARTYING IN THE CHURCH AROUND THE BLOCK FROM THE GHETTO OF MY MIND

I have an alcohol problem, one beer left.

This feeling of daffodils dancing in the sun with dirty,
deranged French poets. It's time to yearn the lusciousness of silk,
the lusciousness of being a man and get up and maybe
just sit back down and rethink fire. The candle flame growl inspires
my mouth to dream past horizons. Past one too many times waking
up in someone else's clothing on a bench making believe a tree is a
nightstand. I hang my keys there. You rethink arson.
It's the only thing waking me up at night. You wonder is a blue sky
as important as a fading fire? The blues of the clouds admit only
to the sun.

MARRIED TO DIVORCE

Out of respect for my wife
I always take my wedding ring off
before I finger another.

Such pride we take
in our
squirming sky birth
boars the ages pieces of paper
with 2 signatures honor and respect.

So don't worry love,
none of those shall apply tonight
and I won't lose my wedding ring inside you.

It's in my left breast pocket

where all marriage yearns to be.

21 JUMP STREET

My teeth are grinding and I keep biting my lips
trying to not think of the possibilities
so I just start focusing on this lightening bug
inside the Bowery Poetry Club
and then somehow all right.
I use vicodin pills like chalk on blackboards
to solve mathematical evasions, entrepreneuative dance
and Velvet Underground smoking Muddy Waters
is what a few vicodin do to me, calmly.
Gets me not wanting greater dantic danger out there but it feels like it could
be the new dantic danger out there or I can't tell, I'm high on vicodin
and sober seizures get me high waking up on the floor but I've been
promising the morning a better Thomas than this. Sober seizure madness.
(My diagnosis) I've been trying to be this Thomas but sometimes it's
easier to play the other Thomas which has more substance and better lines
but then there's the other Thomas who tears a lot but covers it with t-shirts
and matching sneakers or the Thomas who would run for president but can't
because he has asthma and poetry
(my diagnosis)

2 half pills of vicodin

fills missing tooths 18 and 31.

I laugh to myself.

I think the lightning bug saw me.

I don't think I'll ever be able to feel what it's like to be in love again.

(AN 87 PART POEM IN 2 PARTS)

I

Breathing is fundamental.
It's fundamentally sound
to right poems about poetry
because French surrealism is pretty bad ass
and it's the ponderfication of what the poem really is.
Stroke it. Maybe it'll tell you
which direction you want my tongue to finger the clit of your soul.
Some poems, I feel like I'm just playing with the clit
but I tend to think my mistakes are pleasure and pleasure is a
   warm saucer of milk coaxing the stomach
into really believing in yourself but the stomach belches a
   satisfaction, I'm done. I'm a poet.
It's true because I wrote it down and French surrealism is truly
   bad ass in the face of losing the reader
believing in saucers of warm milk.

II

And my mistakes, my mistakes. They're apparent in every
   poem forgotten to make 'em again
and I've seen enough Bounty paper towel commercials to know
   how to clean my messes
but when will it stop? When will it become something you only
   write about?
When will it become a reflection? When will it become a
   forgotten poem?
Poems are written for the ugly because the beautiful have
   no imagination.
Poems are written for the beautiful because the ugly have
   no imagination
Surrealism is truly bad ass. I must be a poet. My nipples are
   tender and sore.

SOMETIMES I THINK WE SHOULD HAVE HAD THE KID

then I wouldn't be up here reading what's more
important poetry, family, drugs or sneakers?
or all encompassing line breaks that seem to
signify the sullen thought ringing in a new year
of hope, dandelions and baby's breath. But I'm here
now, trying to create something is easier then you
think it's just that will to live up to the expectation
signifies the awakening of another grip the tail end
of that thought. Deepen your browns knowing
that rattle comes from your stomach. It just
feels like poems.

THIS POEM

This poem is about my cock. I call him Richard Nixon.
Protruding through the lullabies of disenchantment and revelry with a tongue
of almost forgiveness. He always ensued panic attacks
the panicked for engaging in the debate of rational.
Nixon is the reason that slut knife ran away with that shiny pimped out spoon.
He was the Lucy holding the Balls of America in the palm of his hand
and squeeze ripeness tears. Nixon hates seeing people cry and people cry
the most with begotten truth so Nixon avoided that as much as possible like
3rd period geometry teachers who wanted back rubs.
Nixon's rhetoric,
You know the problem with the blacks . . . ,
You know the problem with the women . . .
You know the problem with the Asians . . .
You know the problem with the Hispanics . . .
You know the problem with the gays . . .

Well I have my own rhetoric . . .
you know the problem with the triple chinned
oily tanned old white muthafuckers it's the constant breeding and tossing
and inheriting originality just to make it the same as originality double dutching
the notion of originality building this mammoth difference elephanated beast
prowling the night persecuting originality.

Nixon claims,
"You have to have a heart to be president and you have to have a head, to control that heart."

But with Nixon's haircut how can the heart really take the head seriously
and how can the head take the body seriously rolling out the door?
Nixon was a man who believed in separating the heart from the head according to
all those Vietnam War documentaries I've seen and the
decapitated heads became
property of the president and advised him.

As I mentioned before this poem is about my cock and I call her truth.
No I'm lying, this poem is about my cock and I call him monster, underneath the bed.
For me Nixon shall always be the bed underneath the monster laughing and I only
wish Nixon was really Pinocchio because then I would have enough wood to make
this fire last.

Then my cock resigned from public office.

Then came the shooting of John Lennon

and then the 80's.

DEAD PAN FATIGUE

We remind each other of poems we write.
White fish on dry rye bookmarks nonsense
on the side of love but love doesn't need help
just cultivation, determined to engorge itself
into pop fluffy red coat zipper shriek madness
representing the passiveness of a sycamore tree
being beaten with a lead pipe.

We remind our poems of each other
and love, love doesn't need help
all love needs is a lead pipe.

(↕)

THOMAS, THE SURGEON

Listen nurse, nurse please stop.
Na na na na na na nurse,
don't want to hear it, stop,
listen, take in, if he has a question
give him a pill. If he has another
question give him another pill.
I think you get it . . . ahhh nurse
I don't want to hear it, now I'll
be in my office and I am not to
be interrupted again, I'm listening
to sea shells.

BLACK
EYED
SEIZURES

I think my skull is shaped differently now.
A lot more pockets and ashtrays
embedded in the bone and thick of it.
The tail end of it.
Has dismemberment changed your life?
Shall your flocked Lego head of hair
recover an ice age
to numb out the beating?
What will the earth remember about me?
The shape of the world is changing
and my skull, my skull
got no time like no time has the fire.

DRUG COUNSELING MEETINGS LATELY

I'm really as gentle and giving as a lady bug.
A deranged manipulative lady bug who enjoys leather studded
  poems
and fiber optic nonsense.
What's your sign
of these times is as stagnant as the morning air on a Monday.
Honesty has gotten me nowhere
honestly
I want to present my self as a particular on this planet of nuanced
assimilation and medium fried
the way things are is not that difficult to assimilate too
but difficulty and ignorance are the only types of clothing that
  fit me
showing off my robustness and scaled back flaws.

Jared and Start keep proclaiming that *they want to swallow*
            the shit out of me
but swallowing me won't get ya high
just a little bloated and lost.
You'd be surprised at what I can't do.
It's difficult deciding if I want a line of poetry or a line of coke.
I rely on bathroom stalls for insight.
Sometimes I'll write a poem or unfoil some white
ladies of the evening open air desire shall be the end of me
and the beginning of another typical Thomas poem.
I've been going to drug counseling meetings lately.
They're the same as poetry open mics
except they have doughnuts and coffee.

I SEE IT IN MY SISTER

eyes of wide

          eyes of could be
prophet or check out girl at Duane Reade.

It doesn't matter as long as those eyes pass the horizon
find that sky screaming blue all comes into focus
inhabiting her pale brown rhododendron eyes
that only bloom when day dreaming. I often pass
through this world never understanding growth.
You will though. I wilt though. You are the next
stage of me, a soft, sophisticated, rich, poem.

INHERITING LIGHT IS LIKE A SOFT HALO OF CRAZINESS EVERYONE'S GOT ONE BUT NO ONE CAN HEAR IT

Fudge you, i'm out of my mine and the blood don't focus like that.
It reiterates the words waiting
for the write vein to pour a glass of red wine
discontent
and bloody, bloody
margarita shots
cause its splits-ville
and the applause and the sounds circle an ever softening halo to drown free
but i could never quite get over the sound of blood
that constant drip
stained home
of a temple
margins the forehead
splattered
with the utmost eloquency and demeanor.
I hear the sound of blood that constant poem
smeared on the floor by your feet
and you often think white bunny rabbits.

Please

fluffy

soft

white

bunny

rabbits.

THOMAS AND THE PURPLE CRAYON

So there was no moon in the sky
so he drew one and then a house
with some windows, a door, a kitchen, a table
and then a mother and a father.

The first time I told my parents I have a cocaine problem
they looked at me odd
like I just told them I want to run for the presidency
or
be an Olympic javelin thrower
or
become a poet.

Thomas draws disappointment on their faces.

Something is about to change in Thomas and I don't even know it.

I hope the need for coke becomes the need for my parents.

The drawing of the house still, stands.
This time Thomas adds shutters to the windows
so nobody can see in or out.

Thomas erases forks, knives and other sharp objects for
protection. He draws a hot air balloon in case he needs to escape.

The 4th time I told my parents I have a cocaine problem
they looked at me sorrowingly, morningly set sunset vibrant
just for a second, gone. Ultimatums fly like thrown high heeled shoes
at my head, rightfully so. Thomas draws band aids. Don't worry
he draws a hot air balloon in case he needs to escape.

I've started writing poems where my father is the course
 through my veins
my mother a circulatory system of never ending branches reaching,
pulsating through arteries bloody blossoming through those
 little veins
in your eyeballs holding a stare of hope. Thomas draws his
 eyelids shut.

The 7th time I told my parents I have a cocaine problem
they looked expected. Expected like the sun.
Expected like one day I would have to put my crayons away.
Expected like no hot water in my building.

Thomas draws mountains of regret
throws them off the George Washington Bridge
if only to draw anew.

I've started drawing these poems
where Thomas is writing about telling my parents about the
 first few times
I had a cocaine problem but they keep coming out like this poem.

Some people call me a drug poet.

My parents are taking the place of drugs in all my poems.

I think
this is a good thing.
I
draw
a smile.

IT'S BEAUTIFUL

if you let it.
it's not love
unless it's 3rd degree assault
and separation
and the poems grow wild
cradled of words like passion,
hold, once and had.
now it's a phone call here
a pain in my side there
and you believe in yourself
one   last   time
and you forget you got you here
and then it crumbles again.
you know it was never love.
it was never 3rd degree assault
it was just a patch of lilies.
humming

I WAS CUT OUT

to be conceived, born
applied pliers of opening wounds wombed and pulsing.
Mesmerize
the incantation
of stealing feeling pulses and ripping out the moon of a Monday
and calling it son.
I react like an almost rattle of something moving belly bound
  robustness
by moving muscle to muscle polar fixed fire.
Do I resemble pulse bound heartbeats often mother
finds reproach in the slight moving to and fro feeling
illusionary, sentencing matter fertile
bound respire pulse.
I am what my mother gave me
and I am what my mother made me
and what mother made me had to be ripped out.

(Inspired by I was not cut out to be conceived
by Jane Ormerod)

THE FLOWERS IN FRONT OF THE BODEGA REMIND ME OF YOU

Remind me blossom brighter than we ever could.

The flowers in front of the bodega
where Moreno put the twenty bags of coke so you would never see the hand off.

Those flowers in front of the bodega
remind me of how your hair used to smell and how love requited rainbows
are for lovers in love.

Oh those flowers
nestled between the thighs and rivers of drug induced fucking emotion.

Those flowers in front of the bodega
are there to remind me that you often invade my thoughts
and the twenty bags of coke behind the flowers in front of the bodega
are there to remind me that i was never even really there.

FLOATING IN A JAR

the night breathes stars
glowing
a trance
to let liquid feel linger through
and post your sign no being
and i shall sing my cries to the heights
of the belly achin' cerebrum and per chance
dream of better control than this.

ask an angel not for the time
just a whisper of help
a whimper of hell
and i'll be there, waiting
with blade in one hand
immortal flying being in the other.

we both breathe hard
then i feel a blade enter my back
and it is god and it is beautiful.

THOMAS, THE SURGEON

We almost lost him.

What a damn shame if he would have
went out like that but hey that's what
I'm here for to control the flux of positive
and negative pigmentations of chemicals
circling your cervix spiting up your spine
head back, pupils hide, nose weeps and
then I get involved. I give that nudge
back to the positive again and the church
chimes, the weddings bell, the moon dances
and we find ourselves, alone in this world
in this influx of time and matter stopping
for a moment to allow him life back into
this room. My advice to him would be
if you want to get off coke, start dating 17 year olds.

EYEBALL PING PONG POLO MADNESS

another sober thought
after fist fucker's anonymous
but it's here and there mutating
when sober.

when sober
wedding rings seem reasonable
and the only addiction
is the closing of one's eye
to impart the other.

i cannot find the blue birds of flying
in these words smother out and ash
this ink rises only to let out a yearning
to numb to even understand.

SOME KIND OF SOBER POEM OR HARMONIOUS DROWNING OR CAN YOU STILL HEAR MY VOICE?

Sitting on my stoop picking my lip with a safety pin.
I want a piece of the night sky with stars on top
but the sun keeps bright without sense appeal
and the blue sky gives such good cloud
and shows art-toons like me on their stoops
wondering how long is long when sober.
We are the unwatered grains of the culture
pleasance.
Hot hostile made for TV movie gunshots rip
through my subconscious' spleen.
A shopping mall dies inside me
but my poems have plenty of other places to steal from
and I realize that even the underground
has nice polished tiles and I want an i-Phod
so I can call you at anytime and let you know
I'm just sitting on my stoop
wondering
if I didn't call
can you still heal my voice?

LAYERING IN MY OWN FILTH

i'm laying in my own filth
it's tiring, boring, dolent of night's stare and frustrated
that it would even perceive to be seen.
i'm sanctioning the light only to siphon a little of my own in a jar
on my end table, glowing.

i'm learning in my own filth
desire, desires, disassurning discourse pressed against the heart beat
and we call it the palm, open.
i allow my self to enter only if entering is never leaving.

i'm turning in my old filth
and my stomach twists a little looser, not so wound just worried
where the storm will hatch
and should i catch it or give it away like a cookie?

i'm writing in my filth
because you won't put them in your poems
so they're gonna have to just be in my poems wandering
hoping the avalanche persuades me to think big, react small
   and hope.

i'm dreaming in my own filth
for you to come back to me but losing it rarely does so you
   drift, faintly, light steps.

i'm dreaming in my filth
roman cathedral tall pointed to the heavens so cherished in
   books of lore
and to the heaven found
in my heart under my bed sheets, away from you all.

(I'VE SEEN MY HEART ENOUGH)

Ahhhh to be young, Mayan and in love again.
To present the beat of my heart again.
The pulse shatters moods into nickel bags of jelly
and everyone steps all over 'em and the molding
'round the words don't care, same old thing, la-di-da-di
bliss and grows this offering of inside me to you.
Ahhhh to be Mayan, young and in love again.
To pound my chest for you.
To decapitate wild boar for you.
To walk barefoot in the forest with only
the twig set soil beneath our cold, clammy feet with you.
To have my chest ripped open
with you.

I FEEL AN ALONENESS COLD WAY,

way, way nestled warming.
The temperate stream
of irrational blossom
like cherry bodega red
induces a shiver,
not quite right.
But my son keeps talking
about his math test thing
or something and I just don't care
feeling creep crawl sprawled out
and rift toe through seldom flight
and who fucking cares about
the debate team, Justin,
Don't you understand?
I feel alone
even married and kids alone.
I could never say that to him
so grin and grim this grime welt
smile purely ghost.
I kindle like ideas
and smother like metaphor showers
and wish he would stop talking
and let me have this silence
but being alone is convincing
everyone you have found.

I WAS DRUNK AND LOST MY TURTLE

an expedition of the mind is expected
to relieve the anxiety of the loss
and a gain in the knowledge
of not always finding amphibious shelled creatures
or the ones you love.

DRIPS OF YOUR INNER THIGH

The duality of man
drips off your inner thigh.

The notion of coming together
breaking apart, the argument

of your hips clefts the tongue
and your inner most demons

rest on the laurels of afterthoughts
and morals way to dark

to scrutinize between the thighs
the duality of man lies

and lies and comes the beginning
of a soft roar.

CHILDREN ARE TIMELESS

(After the 14-year-old from Staten Island who slit his mother's and 3 sisters' throats and then set them all on fire and I know there is new evidence pointing to the mother as the killer but fuck it, I'm sure somewhere, someplace there is a child out there who is about to kill their family.)

You slit their throats and gave them time to breathe.

We have so many helmets and cups protecting children
from the horribleness of life but we have nothing to protect
ourselves from the horribleness of children.

Believe in the children.

Believe in the Easter Bunny.

Believe in the fruit of the tree dropping apples
like ball sacs after making love and hemorrhage
the moment we all find beauty in all this.

Children are the next dreamers, fortune tellers, rapists,
   Dairy Queen moppers,
parents, dictators, wife beaters, husband beaters, firemen, poets,
   open ended sentences,
elitists, and hospital attendant murderers.

They are as guilty as we are.

We should believe in today.

The only time today matters
is tomorrow's documentaries
about yesterday's aspirations.

You slit their throats and gave them time to bleed.

Children don't understand the oceans we die for.

They seem to understand the notes and how to play
a blade across one's throat like a cellist gripping
the neck of the mothers we love.

Cling to wisdom like your remote.

Children are no more timeless than broken clocks.

They will devour you.

I hope the hope of all hope to see us all pedestal strong
raising our hands in flight of one another's glow
but we keep giving birth to these little things that like
to
kill.

Dress them like vases raise them like fire

kill them like weeds

before our children's children

kill our children.

Kill the children.

Save the planet.

Believe in today.

FOR A LITTLE WHILE THERE

i forgot

i existed

excitement

of possibly

a speck

of nothing

inspiration

a lone long

glowne gleam

of sunlight

hits a pond

just right

or the other

just then

gone.

PHOTO: MING CHAN

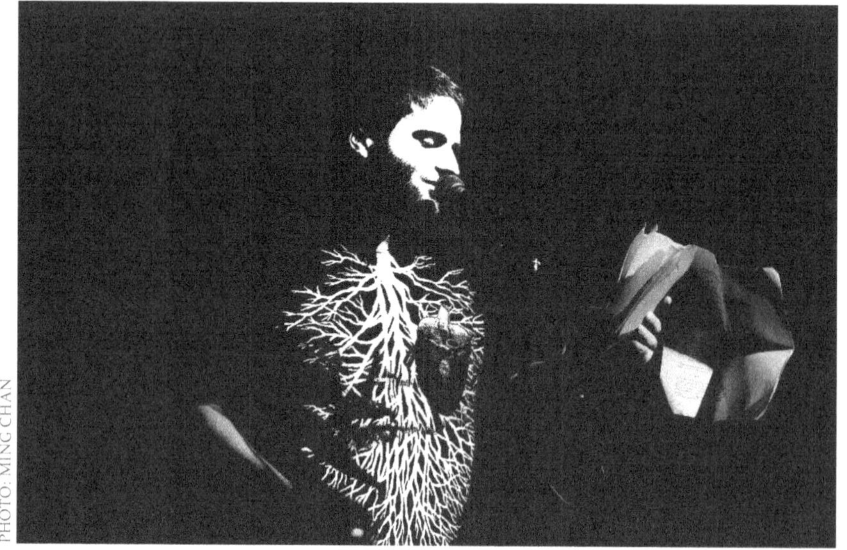

About Thomas Fucaloro

Born in Brooklyn, raised on Staten Island, now resides in Harlem, poet Thomas Fucaloro has survived 3 out of 5 boroughs. He is a graduate of New School University and is a junior editor at New York-based Uphook Press.

ALSO ON THREE ROOMS PRESS

POETRY

by Peter Carlaftes
DrunkYard Dog
Drive By Brooding
I Canto Cantos
Nightclub Confidential
Progressive Shots
Sheer Bardom
The Bar Essentials

by Ryan Buynak
Enjoy the Regrets
Yo Quiero Mas Sangre

by Joie Cook
When Night Salutes the Dawn

by Thomas Fucaloro
Inheriting Craziness is Like a Soft Halo of Light

by Kathi Georges
Bred for Distance
Punk Rock Journal
Slow Dance at 120 Beats a Minute

by Karen Hildebrand
One Foot Out the Door
Take a Shot at Love

by Matthew Hupert
ism

by Dominique Lowell
Sit Yr Ass Down or You Ain't gettin no Burger King

by Jane Ormerod
Recreational Vehicles on Fire

by Susan Scutti
We Are Related

by Jackie Sheeler
to[o] long

by The Bass Player from Hand Job
Splitting Hairs

by Angelo Verga
Praise for What Remains

by George Wallace
Poppin' Johnny

PLAYS

by Madeline Artenberg & Karen Hildebrand
The Old In-and-Out

by Peter Carlaftes
Triumph For Rent (3 Plays)

by Larry Myers
Mary Anderson's Encore
Twitter Theater

HUMOR

by Peter Carlaftes
A Year on Facebook

FICTO-MEMOIR

by Ronnie Norpel
The Constitution Blues

THREE ROOMS PRESS
NEW YORK | threeroomspress.com

www.ingramcontent.com/pod-product-compliance
Lightning Source LLC
Jackson TN
JSHW020713181125
94209JS00008B/4